CW00732177

Thomas Jones of Tregaron
alias
Twm Siôn Cati

Thomas Jones of Tregaron
alias
Twm Siôn Cati

Margaret Isaac

Best wishes

Margaret Isaac

APECS Press
Caerleon

Copyright © 2009 Margaret Isaac

First published in 2009 by APECS Press

The right of Margaret Isaac to be identified as the Author
of this work has been asserted by her in accordance with
the Copyright, Design and Patents Act 1988

*All rights reserved. No part of this publication may be reproduced,
stored in a retrieval system, or transmitted in any form or by any means
(other than short excerpts for the purposes of review)
without the written permission of the publisher*

*Editing and design by
APECS Press Caerleon*

The publisher acknowledges the support of the
Twm Siôn Cati Society
in the production of this book.

www.twmsioncati.co.uk

ISBN 978 0 9548940 9 2

Printed in Wales by
Dinefwr Press, Llandybïe, Carmarthenshire, SA18 3YD

To
Dafydd Wyn Morgan
for keeping the legend alive

Contents

Acknowledgements

I WOULD LIKe to acknowledge the courtesy and assistance of the following: The National Library of Wales, Aberystwyth for permission to use extracts from the pedigrees of Gwaethvoed Lord of Cardigan and Richard Prise and Gwen Prise of Gogerthan, copies of the Will of Thomas Jones and one of his poems.

Carmarthen Record Office for permission to use an extract of the pedigree of Sir Walter Rise of Dinevowr, and a translation of part of this pedigree by Terry Wells, archivist.

Cardiff Library for permission to use extracts from the pedigrees drawn up by Thomas Jones and copied from the original manuscript by William Rees in 1851.

Margaret Jones for her illustrations of Tudor Dress, Maypole dancing and the Mari Lwyd party, first published in *The Tale of Twm Siôn Cati*, Margaret Isaac, 2005.

Brian Davies of Hanes Ffwrwm for his advice and assistance on the pedigree of Thomas Jones.

I am also grateful to my husband, Dr. Alun Isaac for editing the book with his usual care and patience.

Preface

SOME TIME between 1530 and 1540, a son was born to a young girl called Catherine. The boy was named Tomos, son of Siôn. He was illegitimate. This boy was destined to become one of the most famous sons of Wales, for he was Thomas Jones of Tregaron, alias the notorious outlaw known as Twm Siôn Cati.

I became fascinated by this character more than twenty years ago and I was particularly interested in the reasons why the time in which he lived would create such an outlaw as Twm Siôn Cati. It became apparent that, in the sixteenth century, the absence of law and order linked with great poverty made Wales a country in which corruption thrived, and the inability to establish a stable, reliable authoritarian system spawned numbers of outlaws. In fact, Wales probably bore a strong resemblance to the Wild West portrayed in the modern American Western.

In this climate, Twm Siôn Cati, the folk hero, survived against the circumstances of his birth, and showed skill and ability in flouting authority, giving him a timeless appeal to people who admired his ability to overcome impossible situations in ways which they might not condone but would secretly envy.

Writers such as T. J. Llewellyn Pritchard have portrayed Twm Siôn Cati as a highwayman, a thief, a magician, a mimic, and a trickster, misplacing him in the eighteenth century, for he actually lived in the time of the Tudors and James I.

Twm Siôn Cati is now an established Welsh folk hero showing the same stubborn and patriotic resistance to oppressive authority as the Scottish folk hero, Rob Roy and the English outlaw, Robin Hood.

The enigma of a link between Thomas Jones of Tregaron and the outlaw Twm Siôn Cati, revolves around the apparent dichotomy between a lawless figure, such as Twm Siôn Cati, and the perceived respectability of the person known as Thomas Jones. The body of fiction that has grown up around the figure of Twm Siôn Cati, the legendary hero seems to be at odds with Thomas Jones of Fountain Gate, genealogist and heraldic bard, known and respected by the Welsh aristocracy, and a man of substance.

The mystery intrigued me and the outcome of my research is this second book, *Thomas Jones of Tregaron alias Twm Siôn Cati*, which describes the life of Thomas Jones from the time of his pardon by Elizabeth I to his death.

I hope you find, as I did, that Thomas Jones of Tregaron proves to be as exciting and enigmatic as his alter ego.

Margaret Isaac
June 2009

A Background to Welsh History in Tudor Times

INTRODUCTION

IN THE TIME of Thomas Jones, life in Tregaron was very hard for the ordinary villager. The people living in the district of Caron were either poor farmers, or they worked in the local lead mines or gold mines. People were downtrodden by harsh and unjust laws. Thieves were hanged, sometimes for minor offences, but people could also have been hanged, deported or imprisoned for continuing to practise old Welsh customs. They were wild and dangerous times in a land of poverty and persecution.

Before Henry VII came to the throne, the Lancastrian dynasty had already imposed many harsh laws. For example, no Englishman could be convicted in Wales by a Welshman; no commorthas or gatherings were allowed; no unauthorised assemblies were permitted; no Welshman, not loyal to the king, was allowed to bear arms or armour in any town, market, church assembly or highway; no Welshman could hold public office in Wales. These measures reduced Welsh people to the status of second class citizens.

HENRY VII

During the Wars of the Roses of the fifteenth century, the Welsh aristocracy had been much involved in the conflict. They supported Henry Tudor and expected him as a man of Welsh ancestry, to advance the interests of Welsh lords, for example, the Stanleys in North Wales, the Vaughan family in Tretower and the Dwnns in Kidwelly.

There was much lawlessness and disorder in Wales at this time, and hostility towards the Lancastrian government was increasing. Wales needed an ally amongst English royalty, England needed Welsh support. So Henry VII was able to enlist the strength of Welsh warriors in his battle against the Plantagenet, Richard III. Henry was born in Pembroke Castle, but spent his early years in Brittany and France.

Henry claimed descent from the Welsh Tudor dynasty, as the grandson of Owen Tudor and Catherine de Valois. Catherine married Henry V, who died at an early age in the Battle of Agincourt. Later the French princess married Owen Tudor. The Welsh began to perceive Henry Tudor as the heir of Owain Glyndŵr. The support he received from Wales was a significant contribution to his success in the Battle of Bosworth field, where Richard III was killed. Richard was a Plantagenet, and Henry showed pride in his Welsh ancestry. So Henry VII became the first king of the Tudor dynasty.

Henry was perceived by the Welsh princes as a Welshman ruling England and Wales. He had succeeded with the full support of his compatriots, he incorporated the Dragon of Wales in his coat of arms, he wished to restore Welsh rights and to repair the ravages of war.

Many Welsh lords received lucrative rewards for their loyalty. Henry's uncle, Jasper Tudor, who was the son of Catherine, widow of Henry V, was created Duke of Bedford, appointed Justiciar of South Wales and granted the lordship of Glamorgan. Rhys ap Thomas was knighted, appointed Steward of Brecknock, Chamberlain of Carmarthen and Cardigan, and Steward of the lordship of Builth. William Gruffudd was appointed Chamberlain of North Wales. Henry's popularity however was short-lived. Later, he was seen by his former Welsh supporters, to have betrayed his inheritance, exploiting his countrymen for his own ends.

At the opening of the Tudor period Wales was no more than a geographical expression. Parts of Wales were administered by English laws; some were under the jurisdiction of the Marcher lords; some districts were Welshries, where native laws and customs were observed. In each case there were different sets of officials whose spheres of jurisdiction were limited. This confusion of laws and legal systems and the multiplicity of administrative units enabled wrongdoers to evade the penalties for their crimes.

The Great Sessions, meant to try many crimes, were frequently held in abeyance, causing these crimes to go untried. Officials took bribes, failed to hold courts, extorted money, wrongfully dispossessed tenants of their property, and embezzled fines.

The devastation caused by the fighting of the fifteenth century had also brought about widespread poverty. There were family feuds; bitterness experienced by those who suffered from the profound social changes taking place and friction caused by conflicting ambitions. Hostility increased between native Welshmen pushing their way to the top and the English officials standing in their way. It was a country where the strong and the unscrupulous prospered.

This was the situation in Wales when Henry VIII succeeded to the throne in 1509. Lawlessness and corruption pervaded the country and Henry VIII set about attempting to restore law and order. The Acts of Union were intended partially to unite the two countries under one legal system.

HENRY VIII AND ROWLAND LEE

In 1534, Henry VIII created Rowland Lee, Bishop of Lichfield and Coventry and, more significantly for Wales, he was appointed Lord President of the Council in the Marches of Wales. His instructions from Henry were the stern repression of crime, the establishment of order and the inculcation of respect for the law in the Principality and the Marches.

Lee had little love for the people of Wales. He was sycophantic and cruel and because of the power bestowed on him, he was fearless and energetic in the pursuit of his objectives. Lee carried out his tasks with obvious zest and zeal, reporting with relish the measures he took to punish criminals. He used torture and, it is said, hanged over 5,000 men within the space of six years. "Better to hang 100 innocent men that let one criminal go free," was said to be his boast.

His utter lack of respect for rank and his single mindedness in the performance of his duties provoked great enmity but his relentless pursuit of criminals and his unflagging efforts to reduce crime made its mark.

A number of laws were passed to put an end to suborning jurors; to set a limit to uncontrolled crossing of the river Severn by night; to prohibit the carrying of firearms, and to make illegal any kind of meetings or gatherings. Hence, celebrations like the May Day Festivals or the Mari Lwyd, would have been deemed illegal.

THE ACTS OF UNION, 1535-1542

The Acts of Union attempted to bring Wales in line with English laws. Welshmen were to adopt the English legal systems, which then entitled them to enjoy the freedoms, rights, liberties, privileges and laws of England The Romans adopted a similar approach by allowing the people of the nations they had conquered the opportunity to become Roman citizens on condition they adhered strictly to the Roman way of life.

From the time of Hywel Dda, Welsh people had divided their land equally among the family, whereas English land passed to the eldest male. Under Henry's Acts of Union, Welsh land was to be inherited according to the English system without division or partition of land.

Courts of law were to be conducted in only one language – English, a knowledge of which was a prerequisite to hold office. Union placed a premium on the mastery of the English language. The Welsh legal system was moved from Wales, and Wales was to be represented in law at the Westminster Assizes.

There was closer and easier contact with England. English markets became more accessible to Welsh produce and Welsh industries, such as Agriculture and Wool, received a transfusion of capital from England. The Anglicisation of the Welsh gentry was accelerated. The Acts of Union increased general prosperity and order into Wales, although, it could be argued, at a great cost to the Welsh identity and its future prosperity and growth.

See Appendix A2 for a comparative timeline of relevant points in the period 1485-1609.

Thomas Jones,
1530-1559

BIRTH AND EARLY YEARS

S OMEWHERE between the years 1530-1532, Thomas Jones was born at Fountain Gate in Tregaron, Mid-Wales. He was the natural son of David ap Madog ap Howel Moethu. His mother called Catherine or Cati, was a natural daughter of Maredydd ap Ieuan ap Robert.

Thomas Jones's family intermarried with the Herberts, the Vaughans of Tyle-Glas and the Clements, Lords of Caron. Henry VII was also related to Jasper Tudor and the Herbert family, making Thomas Jones a relative of Jasper Tudor and a distant cousin of Henry VIII.

The link between Thomas Jones and the legendary outlaw, Twm Siôn Cati is well known. Strangely, records of Jones's early life are scant, almost non-existent, yet the early years of Twm Siôn Cati are well recorded in folk tales. It is only after Twm Siôn Cati's pardon, that the life of Thomas Jones becomes sufficiently interesting to be recorded.

We know a great deal about the history of the period in which Thomas Jones grew up, so that we may claim to know something of the way he dressed, the food he ate, the games he played and the kind of education he might have received.

CHILDHOOD AND YOUTH

Food

Catherine and Thomas lived in a property called Porth-y-Ffynnon, known in English as Fountain Gate. It was a comfortable residence, and, compared with many other people living in Tregaron at the time, Catherine and Thomas lived in relatively comfortable circumstances. It has been assumed that Thomas's father might have given the property to Cati.

The rural town of Tregaron would have produced lamb, pork and beef, from the sheep, pigs and cattle reared on the land. People would have kept chickens, so apart from fresh meat, they would have also enjoyed eggs and milk from the cows. Judging by the way goats feature strongly in Welsh songs and stories, they would have also drunk goats' milk. The people of Tregaron would have drunk beer, cider, mead, milk, and water.

Trefor Jones in his book, *Welsh Folk Customs*, describes a particular dish served during the Mari Lwyd festival:

> "Cakes and apples baked and set in rows on top of each other with sugar in between in a kind of beautiful bowl which had been made for the purpose and had twelve handles. The warm beer was put in the wassail and the friends sat round the circle near the fire and passed the wassail bowl from hand to hand each drinking in turn."

Part of the staple diet would have been bread.

Children's Dress

Men and boys wore tunics over doubloons and stockings, women and girls wore simple dresses; all were made of woollen material. If they could afford them, people wore shoes made of leather.

Schooldays

Ordinary people were taught either by the monks or curates from the church, who were very strict in their discipline. They would think nothing of taking the birch broom to any child who did not conform to their rules. The church also collected tax-money from the local inhabitants. Since the people were very poor and the clergy lived a privileged, comfortable existence, this tax-collecting did not make them very popular!

Schools possessed few books as we know them – the printing press had only just been invented. The hornbooks or battledores, as they were also known, were made of wood and shaped like a table tennis bat, onto which a piece of parchment was secured. On the parchment paper was written the alphabet, vowel sounds and the Lord's Prayer which the children used to recite every day. The more elaborate horn books were protected by a thin sheet of cow's horn and were beautifully decorated.

Many people in Wales were unable to read or write, but when England and Wales were joined together, it became more important to do so. More schools were being set up and ordinary people tried very hard to send their children to school. However, many people were poor and lived off the land, so that sometimes they could not spare their children from working in the fields.

Music

Singing, dancing and playing instruments was an important part of life in Tregaron. Instruments used would have included the harp, the flute and the fiddle. These were played during festivals such as the May Day festival or the Mari Lwyd, and at special occasions such as weddings. Many old Welsh songs have been collected and printed, and some are listed in the select bibliography.

21

So Thomas, his family and his friends might have sung songs such as *Oes Gafr Eto* or *Migildi Magildi*, and his mother might well have sung *Ar Lan y Môr* or *Suo Gân* to her son on quiet winter evenings.

Children's Games

Popular outdoor games in Tregaron would have been running, leaping, rowing, shooting matches with bows and arrows, mock battles with sword and buckler, quarterstaff combats, throwing the bar, and fishing in the Tywi River.

Horse races would have been as popular in Tregaron as they are today, and Thomas undoubtedly enjoyed riding. Trials of strength were also enjoyed especially wrestling matches or a tug-of-war.

Indoor games would have included playing with dice and playing chess. Trefor Jones writes that the game was played by the simplest sort of people skilfully. He also gives some of the names used by Welsh chess players: *Fristol Tawlbwrdd* for the play; *Elphin* was the name for the bishop; Rooks were *Brain Owen ap Urien* and the pawn was *Y Penned Bach*. Another popular game was Backgammon, it has been suggested that the name comes from two Welsh words: *bach* (little) and *cammon* (battle).

Social Customs

We know, too, something of the social customs, such as village seasonal celebrations, traditional games, and social customs. This enables us to continue to build up a picture of the childhood and early years of Thomas Jones. The two major festivals took place at the most important times of the year, summer and winter.

Summer Festivals

These summer festivals were called *Calan Mai* (May Festival) or *Calan Haf* (Summer Festival) and were frequently held on May Day. At the beginning of summer, cattle were moved to summer pastures, servants were hired, and fairs were held. The winter counterpart was called *Calan Gaeaf* (Winter Festival). These festivals divided the year into two calends to celebrate the two dominant seasons of summer and winter.

May Day festivals were forbidden by Henry VIII, since they constituted a considerable gathering of people.

The *twmpath chwarae* was a green generally situated at the top of a hill on ground higher than any which surrounded it. The harpist or fiddler sat on the top of the mound playing music for the dancing and singing of May carols. Sometimes carollers sang in this way from door to door much in the same way as carollers might do at Christmas.

The people assembled at the *twmpath chwarae* for sports and pastimes principally dancing. A harp or a fiddle was played and people dressed in holiday attire. Other activities at the *Twmpath* might include tennis playing, bowling, throwing the stone or beam, and wrestling.

The May Pole was usually made from a birch tree, this was called *Codi'r Fedwen* (raising the birch) in South Wales. May Poles were raised in different parts of the town and young men and women would join together and 'thread the needle', in other words, they would wend their way from one may pole to another till they had traversed the town. The May Pole was usually between twelve to fourteen feet in length and decorated with evergreen, flowers and ribbons.

Mari Lwyd

In Tregaron, in the time of Thomas Jones, harvest meals and gatherings were the usual celebrations at the *Calan Gaeaf*, which began in November. These illegal gatherings would have been rigorously stamped out by Rowland Lee.

Perhaps the most well known and enduring festival known today is that of the Mari Lwyd which celebrated the 'letting in' of the New Year; *Mari* means mare, *Lwyd* means grey. Grey was the colour of the old Celtic religion, it was the colour between black and white, a twilight colour signifying the border between light and darkness. Grey was therefore considered a spiritual colour. Significantly, even today,

white horses in Britain are called greys. The horse was a potent symbol in Celtic mythology and in the Mabinogion.

The Mari Lwyd was a horse's skull, the head having been buried in quick lime or had been kept buried after the previous year's festivities. The lower jaw was fixed with a spring which caused the mouth to open and shut with a loud snap when operated by the person carrying the Mari. A pole about five feet long was inserted into the horse's skull and a white sheet draped over it.

Coloured ribbons were used to decorate the skull and bottle glass was used to represent the eyes; pieces of black cloth were sewn on to the sheet to represent the ears. The man carrying the Mari's head stood underneath the sheet holding the pole and operating the lower jaw with a short handle.

Reins with bells were placed on the Mari's head and held by the leader who carried a stick for knocking at doors. This prowling monster was sometimes carried round and pushed through a window or could be seen creeping around the room!

Members of the party might play instruments like the fiddle. Ribbons on the horse's head and adorning the members of the party were thought to represent tongues of fire or fertility. The Mari Lwyd group moved from house to house. They stood outside each house and sang traditional verses which referred to the Mari Lwyd and asked to be allowed to enter the house.

The people inside the house sang verses in response showing at first their reluctance to let in strangers and seeking reassurances that they would come to no harm. Eventually, the inhabitants were persuaded to allow the Mari Lwyd inside. The company then sat round in a circle near the fire and passed the wassail bowl from hand to hand each drinking in turn. Lastly, the wassail, namely the cakes and ale, was shared among the whole company.

The Mari Lwyd's acceptance into the home symbolised the recognition by mortals of the existence of a spiritual world and the interdependence of the two worlds. The Mari Lwyd progressed in this manner to other houses in the village and performed in the same way. The feeding and drinking also harmonised with the time of year and the traditional hospitality of the Welsh and Celtic people.

The custom has layers of symbolism attached to it. It is a fertility rite, it has a horse, references to hospitality to strangers in winter, the passing of a bowl of food and drink which is associated with the ancient ritual of a cauldron, and the central image of a head, which is reminiscent of the mythology attached to Brân the Blessed.* The fertility motif is substantiated by later attempts to explain the name Mari Lwyd.

The departing song of the party is a kind of fertility blessing that the house may continue to thrive and have children, or that the crops will grow, in other words, that life will continue.**

So, life would have continued in this way, but for Henry VIII's determination to change the laws and join together England and Wales into one geographical and cultural region.

---

* Brân is a giant and king of Britain in Welsh mythology. He appears in the second branch of the Mabinogi, where he makes a gift of a magic cauldron to the king of Ireland. When the dead Irish warriors were placed in it, they came to life and were able to fight as well as ever. Brân is mortally wounded in a later battle and orders that his head be cut off and buried in London. The head was supposed to be able to speak. The talking head is widely considered to derive from the ancient Celtic 'cult of the head'; the head was considered to be the home of the soul.

** Mari Lwyd verses included in Appendix.

Thomas Jones's Life,
1559-1609

PARDON

IN THE time of poverty and persecution endured in Wales in the reign of Henry VIII, Thomas Jones or people like him would have undoubtedly become outlaws.

In 1558, Elizabeth I was crowned Queen of England. After the excesses of the previous reign of Henry VIII, the short reign of his son Edward, and the reign of terror imposed on the country by Henry's daughter Mary, England looked forward to a return to stability under their new young Queen. They were not disappointed. Elizabeth set about restoring unity and harmony in her kingdom and her reign heralded the new Renaissance. Wales had suffered greatly and Elizabeth's first gesture towards her subjects was a general pardon to all those who had, for one reason or another, been forced to act outside the law.

Under this new dispensation, on the 15th January 1559, Thomas Jones, was granted a pardon under the Great Seal, forgiving him *omnia escapia et cautiones*. He was 29 years old.

The Pardon

Thome Johns alias Cattaye nuper de Tregaen in com. Cardigan. Gen. alias diet.

Thome Johns alias Catty ae Tregaen in com. Cardigan, genereso, alias diet.

Thome Johns alias Catty, gent seu quocunque alio nominee vel cognomina seu additione hominis cognitionis dignitatis, office seu losi idem Thomas copiatur, vocetur seu nuncupetur.

For 'omnia escapia et cautiones'.

HERALDRY AND GENEALOGY

Everything we read of Thomas Jones of Tregaron marks him as a respectable, well educated, well connected gentleman. His pedigree connects him with Gwaethvoed, prince of Ceredigion, and he claims kinship with Lord Cecil, through his grandfather Howel Moethu (Appendix A1, A4).

His notable distinction is that of heraldic bard. Some of his contemporaries give him high praise:

'Whoever professes himself to be an heraldic bard, must know the pedigrees of Kings and Princes, and be skilled in the works of three Chief Bards of the Isle of Britain; namely, Merlyn the son of Morvryn, Merlyn Ambrosius, and Taliesin the Chief Bard. And in the Science of Heraldry, with respect to being thoroughly acquainted with the real descents, armorial bearings, dignities and illustrious actions of the nobility and gentry of Wales, the most celebrated, accomplished and accurate (and that beyond doubt), is reckoned Thomas Siôn, alias Moethau, of Porth-y-Ffynnon, near Trev Garon, and when he is gone, it will be very a doubtful chance that he will be able for a long time to leave behind him an equal, nor indeed any Genealogist (with regard to being so conversant as he in that science), that can ever come near him.'

(Dr. John David Rees)

Y godidocaf a phennaf a pherffeithiaf . . . yng nghelfyddyd arwyddfarddoniaeth (the most excellent most impressive and most perfect . . . in the art of genealogical poetry.

(*Grammar, 1592, Siôn Dafydd Rhys*)

Examples of Thomas Jones's work are included below and in the Appendix, A5 (a) (b), A8.

This table doeth shew | how the right wo[l] : S[r] | Water Rise of Newton | in Dinevowr, wth in the | county of Caermarthen | now lyvinge knight is | lineally discended from | Seaven kinges, Five | Dukes, fyfteene Earles, | and twelve Barons : | And but nyne discentes | Betweene him and the | farthest of them : Som wth in eight discentes, | som wth in seaven, som | wth in 6, som 5, som 4, | som 3, and some wth in | two discentes to himself : | As this Petegree -- | mentioneth. | And sett forth by me | Thomas Jones of -- | Tregaron. | Fynished at Fountaine | Date the xxii[th] of | Marche 1605. ---

Vignette from the pedigree of Sir Walter Rise of Newton in Dinevowr.
See also vignette, Appendix 8.
(Translation: courtesy of Carmarthen Record Office).

The Acts of Union passed by Henry VIII compelled Wales to adopt English laws and do away with their own. Antiquarianism and genealogy had always been of interest amongst the Welsh gentry, due to their curiosity about every aspect of learning, including history, literature and religion. After the Acts of Union, genealogy took on a more pragmatic role, due to the English inheritance laws. In England, lands left by the father, became the property of the eldest son, whereas, by the Welsh laws, obtaining before 1535, the land was divided equally between all the sons. This necessitated the compilation of the pedigrees of families who owned much land, and heraldry became a necessary profession.

Thomas Jones proved himself adept at the work, and his services were requisitioned by the chief gentry in his own and bordering counties. He drew up the pedigrees of the great and famous. Among them were Charles Morgan of Arkeston, Herbert, Earl of Pembroke, Ideo Wyllt, Lord of Llywel, Sir Thomas Moston of Moston and Sir Henry Johnes of Abermarles. He also drew up his own pedigree. Many of these genealogies are now kept in the British Museum, the National Library of Wales, Aberystwyth, and one in the Carmarthen Museum. They reflect the work of an accomplished heraldic historian.

POET

Thomas also gained some reputation as a poet during his lifetime. Some evidence suggests that he attended an Eisteddfod at Llandaff as an ordained bard, a few poetic forms such as *cywyddau* and *englynion* are attributed to him. The following poem shown on page 33 (courtesy, National Library of Wales, Aberystwyth) was written by Twm Siôn Cati.

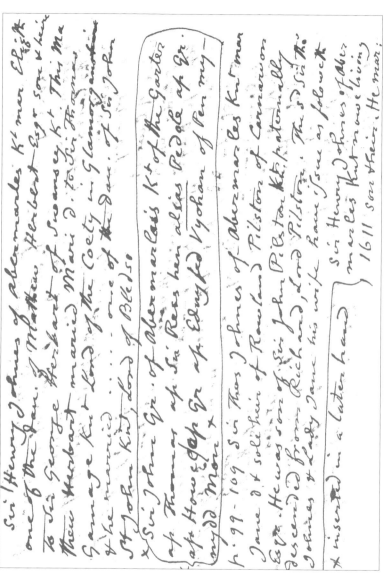

Pedigree of Sir Henry Johnes of Abermarles.

Extracts from Pedigrees of Wales by Twm Siôn Cati transcribed from original mss by Wm Rees, typographum de Llandovery, 1851.
See Appendix A5(b) for the pedigree of Wm. Herbert, Earl of Pembroke.
(Courtesy, Cardiff Central Library).

Copy of an original poem by Thomas Jones.
(Courtesy, National Library of Wales, Aberystwyth).

He was on familiar terms with the poets of his day. A poem by Silas ap Siôn compares the rivalry of Thomas Jones and Dafydd Benwyn over a girl called Ely to the war caused by Helen of Troy! Some of the poems attributed to Thomas Jones are preserved in the British Museum and in the National Library of Wales, Aberystwyth.

LIFE AT FOUNTAIN GATE

After Thomas's pardon he is known to have resided for the rest of his life at Fountain Gate; this property had apparently been built on an old hafod belonging to the Gwaethfoed family. The house has been in ruins for the past couple of hundred years, the only items of historical interest that have been found on the site were three carved stones. They bear some obscure lettering . . .

Thomas Jones married twice. His first wife's name is unknown, but it is recorded in the Fenton MS (housed in Cardiff Free Library) that he had three children, Rees, John and Margaret, who became the wife of William Morgan of Llanfihangel Crucorney. His second wife was Joan (Johane) Williams, daughter of Sir John Price of the Priory of Brecon.

The years passed, with Thomas living the life of a respected country gentleman. His property at Porth-y-Ffynnon included fields of wheat and barley, and he kept cattle so, presumably, he enjoyed the status of a prosperous farmer.

One imagines he would have entertained his friends in Tregaron, and those of note who lived further afield. One person of some interest, living at the time, in London, visited Thomas Jones on more than one occasion. He was his cousin and a man of substance, his name was Dr John Dee.

John Dee was an eminent Elizabethan mathematician and astrologer. His interest in the occult and his many travels abroad gave rise to the suspicion that he was a secret government agent, whose code name was 007. It is possible that the author, Ian Fleming, was aware of the reputation of John Dee, and conceived the idea of using the same code name for his creation, James Bond.

John Dee was born in London in 1527 and was educated at Cambridge. His father was a gentleman server to Henry VIII and John himself claimed to be of Welsh royal descent; John Dee died in 1608.

THE MORGAN DAVYD AFFAIR

After his pardon, dated 15th January 1559, we have some evidence that he was again on the wrong side of the law on a number of occasions. M. R. E. Thomas stated in *Twm Siôn Cati – Truth, Tales and Tradition*, 2003, that in August 1561, his name appeared on the plea roll as a defendant in a Great Session Court in Glamorgan. He is referred to as Thomas Jones alias Cattye de Tregaron. It is stated that he was suspected of felonies. There is more evidence in his later life that he was not quite respectable.

However, his recognition as a poet and heraldic bard in the latter part of the sixteenth century would seem to indicate that Thomas Jones, alias Twm Siôn Cati, had become a respectable member of society. But in 1598, death, danger and drama entered Thomas's life once more.

The Vicar of the parish was a man called Morgan Davyd. It seems that he had impoverished fifty villagers by charging them before the County Sessions to keep the peace. In an article in the *Transactions* of the Carmarthenshire Antiquarian Society (Frederick Jones, 1939), the writer suggests that Morgan Davyd's anger might have been invoked, because Thomas Jones defended the people of the parish against his actions.

In 1601, as Steward of the lordship of Caron, he is plaintiff in a suit for alleged assault against the Vicar and his men. The transcripts by the plaintiff are included in Frederick Jones's article. They have such drama and immediacy as a unique primary source of a chapter in the life of Thomas Jones. They are printed here in full.

> Having forcibly obtained possession of one of Thomas Jones's cornfields, the Vicar caused his horses and cattle to trample upon the wheat and barley. Thereupon John Moythe, a menial servant, "gently desired" the Vicar and his men, Evan Roger and John Davyd, to remove the animals, for already that summer they had damaged £40 worth of corn. But Morgan Davyd, having a sword and dagger at his belt, and a bastinado tipped with a long iron spike in his hand, struck the servant with the latter several times, so that he fell and lay greeving and gasping for life. Then he trod on him, and kicked him into a ditch, putting his arm out of joint.

> Eleanor Pryce, a maid servant, rushed out to rescue the poor fellow; but when she saw the Vicar still there she turned to run home. His men caught her and struck her until she fell unconscious. Some neighbours carried the two victims to Fountain Gate.

> Another day, When Jenkyn the tyler was mending the church, the Vicar tried to stop him. The tyler explained that only the chancel was legally in the Vicar's care. Morgan Davyd hurried home for help. The

tyler rallied his friends. The Vicar was soon back with a great axe and a sword, accompanied by Ieuan Rogers, his son-in-law, who had a main pike, John Davyd with a gleve, and ten other armed men. They challenged the tyler and his friends, who thereupon retreated leaving their ladders to be smashed.

On 9th July, 1598, the Vicar plotted with his brother John Davyd, and Ieuan ap Roger, his son-in-law, to hang John Moythe. They waited till they saw Moythe going to the mountain, then, taking a rope of hair and being armed with long pike staves, gleves, swords, daggers, etc. they crept after him. But he made such a noise when they were dragging him up the tree, that the neighbours hastened to his rescue. The print of the rope remained about his neck for six months.

But worse was to come. On 23rd March, 1599 the Vicar publicly announced "that he would be the death of" Thomas Jones.

Morgan Davyd, Ieuan ap Roger, John Davyd, Ieuan ap Davyd, Gwenllian ap Davyd and others, armed with swords, daggers, long staves, pitchforks, gleves, main pikes and other unlawful weapons marched to the gate of Fountain Gate on 7th April, 1599. They forcibly stopped the servants driving the cattle to a nearby close, attacked the men, and stoned some of the animals to death. When he heard his servants cry for help, Thomas Jones ran out. Forthwith the Vicar, John Davyd and Ieuan ap Roger attacked him with their gleves and pikes, and he would have been killed, if he had not been rescued by his neighbours. He took many months to recover from his wounds and bruises.

On 24th August, 1599, the Vicar and his friends, armed as before, caught one of Jones's animals running down a hill. They took the animal, a calf, to Fountain Gate and there set two mastiffs upon it, hoping that the noise would bring Thomas Jones out. One of the servants, Agnes verch (daughter) Thomas, foolishly ran out.

Gwenllian was ordered to kill Agnes; so she dashed at her with a rake, and cracked her skull. The noise attracted Jones and his men. In the ensuing skirmish, the Vicar rushed at Jones and threw his gleve with such force, that it struck his side, penetrated his doublet and shirt, and sunk three inches into his body. Elynor Pryce, Jones's cousin, attempted to rescue him, but was prevented by Gwenllian, who struck her with a key and broke two of her teeth. Jones and his people retreated to the house and closed the gate. The others tried to break open the gate and enter the house.

Shortly afterwards Thomas Jones took the matter before the Courts. Some time in the year 1600, Rees ap Ieuan Gitto sent his wife and two others to serve the process out of the Court of Exchequer upon the Vicar. When the latter received the process, he threw it on the ground and stamped on it.

On 16th April, 1601, when Jones, as Steward for the Lordship of Caron, was keeping the Leet Court, the Vicar entered with a sharp dagger hidden under his coat. He gradually crept closer to his enemy. Just as he was about to use the weapon, some of Jones's friends saw him, and pushed him away. "And thereupon the said Morgan Davyd presently began to be in a great rage and, most wickedly and ungodly, vowed and protested that he cared not what death he should suffer so that he might speed and kill your said subject."

After the case against the Vicar was heard in the court of Star Chamber, the matter seems to have quietened down. The incidents appear to be somewhat exaggerated, but the details give a clear idea of the depth of the hatred between the two men. From the comments and witness of many of the villagers, Morgan Davyd appears to have attracted much fear and dislike in Tregaron. Tithed vicars were not popular, they exacted tithes or taxes from their parishioners, who were expected to pay in kind, from produce they could ill afford. The description of the feud between Thomas Jones and Morgan Davyd is one-sided, but it gives a fascinating glimpse of life in Tregaron in the last two years of the sixteenth century.

Life became a little quieter for Thomas after this short episode of strife. He continued to produce pedigrees of the landed gentry of Wales and drew up those of Sir Thomas Moston and Sir Henry Johnes of Abermarles in 1604. During this time he was also Justice of the Peace.

Last Days

THOMAS was now 74 years of age and life was not yet over for him. He began to show interest in the Lady of Ystradffin. Her name was Joan, daughter of Sir John Price of Brecon Priory and wife of Thomas ap Rhys Williams, a wealthy landowner who had been High Sheriff of Cardigan, Brecon and Carmarthen. Ystradffin was 12 miles from Fountain Gate on the road from Tregaron to Llandovery and Brecon.

It is highly likely that Thomas and Joan had met on social occasions. Their marriage was preceded by a strange set of circumstances. Joan's husband died in 1607 soon after making his Will. Thomas Jones then helped Joan and her brother-in-law to alter her late husband's Will, so that she could retain £200 worth of gold and silver jewellery, although the Will gave her over £3,000 of land and goods – a tremendous fortune in those days. Very soon after Thomas married Joan, the executors of the Will complained before the Star Chamber that "Thomas Jones et Joan uxor, late wife of the said Thomas Williams" had falsified her late husband's Will, and detained his goods.

Two years later, at the age of 79 years, Thomas Jones died. The heiress of Ystradffin possessed lands worth £200 per annum, goods and chattels worth £3,000, and £2,000 in jewellery. It is not surprising that this old lady should be much sought after. Shortly after Thomas's death she married Sir George Devereux.

Thomas Jones's Will is held at the National Library of Wales, Aberystwyth. In it he made a bequest of nine cattle to his 'base son' John

Moythe, and the residue of his estate to his 'loving wife' Johane.* In his death, he remains an enigma. Describing John Moythe as his 'base son' is an acknowledgement of an illegitimate child. Who was the mother? What story lies hidden there?

Even more of a mystery is the manner of his death. A rumour exists that he was murdered by Johane and her third husband Sir George Devereux. Devereux had forfeited all his property to the Crown, and was living quietly as a tenant at Llwynybrain near Llandovery, and Sir George did prosper from his marriage to the twice enriched heiress of Ystradffin.

There is a well known legend attached to Ystradffin concerning a bloodstain said to be still visible on the floor of one of the bedrooms of the house. The legend has slipped into one of the stories linked with Twm Siôn Cati. He is said to have fallen in love with the heiress of Ystradffin and wooed her during many visits from his cave nearby at Rhandirmwyn. On one such visit, he stood outside the window, and proposed marriage. She had promised to marry him, but was now refusing his proposal, so he grabbed her hand and threatened to cut it off, if she did not keep her promise! The alleged bloodstain in the house is offered as evidence that the tale is true.

The records show that Thomas Jones married a mature widow when he was 77 years of age, so at the very least, the apocryphal story seems to be strangely prophetic in the light of the later marriage of Thomas Jones. A more credible solution may be that the rumours which circulated about the murder of Thomas by his wife somehow got mixed up with the fictional tales of Twm Siôn Cati.

---

* Full copy of Thomas Jones's Will can be seen in the Appendix A6 (a) (b) (c) (Welsh), A7 (a) (b) (English).

The last mystery of Thomas Jones remains unsolved. The whereabouts of his burial place are unknown.

Thomas Jones, alias Twm Siôn Cati, has attracted a plethora of documents, stories, and hypotheses regarding his life and identity. Born at a time of historical upheaval in Wales, a time of oppression and lawlessness, he contributed much to his home at Tregaron. He was a caring landowner, employing many people on his farmland, he was a family man, he was an educated man, he enjoyed writing and was proud of his ability to produce pedigrees of the famous men of Wales. He was highly respected by the people of Tregaron, who conferred on him the Stewardship of Caron. He was also known for acting on the 'windy' side of the law throughout his life.

The ambiguity of the man who is seen as Twm Siôn Cati and Thomas Jones does perhaps represent the upheaval of the social times in which he lived. Thomas Jones, alias the outlaw Twm Siôn Cati, had been compelled like many men to live his early life outside the laws imposed on Wales by the Acts of Union, and, perhaps even more so when Queen Mary ascended the throne. She set out to re-establish the Roman Catholic religion in a particularly vicious and bloody manner.

It may be that Thomas Jones was a son of Tregaron coerced into leading a double life, in particular during the reign of Mary. His pardon was given by Elizabeth under a general amnesty, which she intended to help to re-establish harmony in the country, after Mary's reign. Thomas Jones is pardoned for *omnia escapia et cautiones* which suggests that he had operated outside the law but not to any great extent. Many outlaws roamed the district around Tregaron and it is possible that Thomas Jones became associated with the misdemeanours and subterfuges of such men for which he was not himself responsible.

Certainly many apocryphal tales have created a rascal, a figure of fun and a caricature of the original folk hero.

Perhaps he was a man who used his wits to survive in the most wild and dangerous times in Wales. Perhaps it is time to recognise his fortitude, his intellect and his love of life and salute a Welsh folk hero who stands for a necessary expression of the spirit of an oppressed people.

Bibliography

Anon: *Ogof Twm Siôn Cati*, Dinas RSPB Reserve, 1985.

Barber, Chris: *Mysterious Wales*, Blorenge Books, 2000.

Barber, Chris: *More Mysterious Wales*, David and Charles, 1986.

Borrow, George: *Wild Wales*, Collins, 1977.

Crow, Barbara: *Children's Reading Books from 1534 to 1780*, M.Ed. Dissertation, University of Wales, Aberystwyth, 1987.

Davies, R. Isgarn: *Twm Shôn Gati*, Cardiganshire Antiquarian Society Trans., Vol. 5, 1927.

Evans, Gwynfor: *Land of my Fathers*, Y Lolfa, 1992.

Evans, John Gilbert: *Llyfr Hwlangerddi y Dref Wen*, Gwasg y Dref Wen, 1981.

Fielding, Henry: *The Adventures of Tom Jones*, Penguin, 1954.

Gwyndaf, Robin: *Welsh Folk Tales*, National Museum of Wales, Cardiff, 1992.

Harries, Frederick: 'The Welsh Elizabethans Customs and Games', *Glamorgan County Times*, 1924.

Hughes, Lynn: 'Is Twm the Real Tom Jones?' *The Western Mail Weekend Magazine*, 4th August 1973.

Hughes, Lynn: *Hawkmoor*, Swansea, 1977.

Jenkins Dafydd: *Hywel Dda: The Law*, Gomer Press, 1986.

Jones, Beryl M.: *Further Adventures of Twm Shôn Catti*. Book No. 4 reprint, Western Mail and Echo Ltd.

Jones, J. Frederick: *Thomas Jones of Tregaron alias Twm Sion Cati*, Carmarthenshire Antiquarian Society Transactions, 1939, pp. 77-87.

Meyrick, Samuel Rush: *The History of Cardiganshire Hundred of Penarth*, Davies & Co., 1907.

Owen, Trefor: *Welsh Folk Customs*, Gomer Press, 1987.

Prichard, T. L.: *The Surprising Adventures of Twm Shôn Catti, A Wild Wag of Wales*, David Davies, Ferndale.

Rees, F. Walter: 'Will of Twm Siôn Catti, A.D. 1609', *The Cardigan Herald*, August 18, 1918.

Rhys, John: *Celtic Folklore Welsh and Manx*, Oxford, 1901.

Scott, Sir Walter: *Rob Roy*, Penguin, 1995.

Stephens, Meic: *The New Companion to the Literature of Wales*, University of Wales Press, Cardiff, 1998.

Thomas, Hugh: *A History of Wales 1485-1660*, University of Wales Press, 1972.

Thomas, Mathew Robert Ewan: *Twm Siôn Cati*, M.A. Aberdeen, 2000.

Website Wikipedia

    Tudor Dress.

    Rural way of life in early 16th century.

    Food in early 16th century esp. spices, sugar.

    The use of glass in early 16th century.

Appendix

A1   *Front Cover:* Vignette from the pedigree of Gwaethvoed, Lord of Cardigan by Thomas Jones. (Courtesy: National Library of Wales, Aberystwyth).

A2   A Comparative History Timeline.

A3   Verses of the Mari Lwyd by Dafydd Dafis, Maesteg, from the Parish of Llangynwyd.

A4   Extract from the *Heraldic Visitation of Wales and Part of the Marches* Lewys Dwnn, ed. Meyrick Samuel Rush, 1846. (Courtesy: National Library of Wales, Aberystwyth).

A5(a)   Vignette from the pedigree of Richard Prise of Gogerthan and Gwen Prise his wife by Thomas Jones. (Courtesy: National Library of Wales, Aberystwyth).

A5(b)   Extract from the pedigree of Wm. Herbert, Earl of Pembroke. (Courtesy: Cardiff Central Library).

A6(a)   Copy of 1st part of Thomas Jones's Will. (Courtesy: National Library of Wales, Aberystwyth).

A6(b)   Copy of 2nd part of Thomas Jones's Will. (Courtesy: National Library of Wales, Aberystwyth).

A6(c)   Copy of 3rd part of Thomas Jones's Will. (Courtesy: National Library of Wales, Aberystwyth).

A7   Translation of Thoms Jones's Will. (Courtesy: The Kite Centre, Tregaron).

A8   *Back Cover:* Extract from the pedigree of Sir Walter Rise of Newton in Dinevowr by Thomas Jones. (Courtesy: Carmarthen Record Office).

Vignette from the pedigree of Gwaethvoed, Lord of Cardigan by Thomas Jones

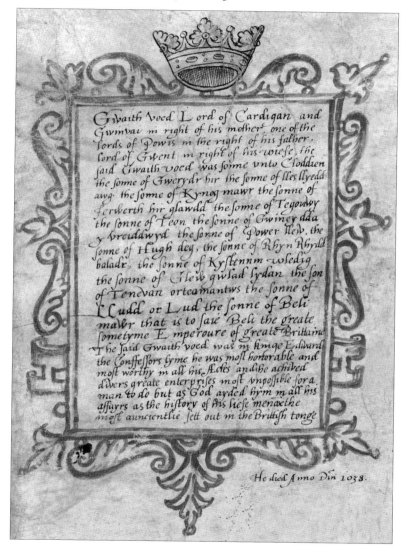

Gwaith Voed Lord of Cardigan and Gwmvai in right of his mother, one of the lords of Powis in the right of his father, lord of Gwent in right of his wiefe, the said Gwaith voed was fonne vnto Cloddien the fonne of Gwerydr hir the fonne of lles llyedd awg the fonne of Kynog mawr the fonne of ferberth hir glawdd the fonne of Tegowwy the fonne of Teon the fonne of Gwiney dda y vreuddwyd the fonne of Power llew, the fonne of Hugh deg, the fonne of Rhyn Rhydd baladr, the fonne of Kyftennm wledig the fonne of Glew gwlad fydan the fon of Tenevan orteamantws the fonne of Cudd or Lud the fonne of Beli mawr that is to fair Beli the greate fometyme Emperoure of greate Brittaine The faid Gwaith voed was in kinge Edward the Conffeffors tyme he was moft hortorable and moft worthy in all his Actes and the achived divers greate enterprifes moft vnpoffible for a man to do but as God ayded hym in all his affayrs as the hiftory of his liefe menaethe moft auncientlie fett out in the Brittifh tonge

He died Anno Din 1038.

A Comparative History Timeline

Welsh History, 1485-1559	Thomas Jones (Twm Siôn Cati), 1530-1609	English History, 1485-1603
1485 The Battle of Bosworth Field.	**1530** Born at Fountain Gate, the natural son of David ap Madog ap Howel Moethu, by Catherine, a natural daughter of Maredydd ap Ieuan ap Robert. His family inter-married with the Herberts, the Vaughans of Tyle-Glas and the Clements, Lords of Caron. Henry VII was also related to Jasper Tudor and the Herbert family).	**1485** The Battle of Bosworth Field.
1493 Arthur made Prince of Wales.		Henry VI son of Henry V and Catherine de Valois (who later married Owain Tudor).
1521 Duke of Buckingham executed. He had contributed to the victory in 1485.		**1509** Henry VII dies and Henry VIII becomes King of England.
1531 Rhys ap Griffith executed. He had contributed to the victory in 1485.		Henry VIII son of Henry VII and Elizabeth of York.
		1509 Henry m. Catherine of Aragon.
1534 Rowland Lee appointed Bishop of Lichfield and Lord President of the Marches of Wales.	**1534** Twm is 4 years old when Rowland Lee is made Bishop of Lichfield.	**1516** Mary I born.
		1533 Henry m. Anne Boleyn.
		1533 Elizabeth I born.
Acts of Union **1534 and 1543**.	**1534-1543** Twm 4-13 years of age during Lee's reign of terror in Wales.	**1536** m. Jane Seymour.
		1537 Edward VI born.
1543 Rowland Lee died.		**1540** m. Anne of Cleves.
1547 Henry VIII died.	**1547** Twm 17 years of age when Henry VIII died.	**1540** m. Catherine Howard.
		1543 m. Catherine Parr.
1547-1553 Edward IV country still Protestant.	**1547-1553** Twm 17-23 years of age during Edward IV's reign.	**1547** Edward IV crowned King of England.
		1553 Mary I crowned Queen of England and Ireland.
1553-1558 Queen Mary country changed to R.C. again.	**1553-1558** Twm 23-28 years of age during Mary's reign.	**1554** Mary I m. Philip of Spain.
		1558 Mary I died childless and Elizabeth I crowned Queen of England.
1558 Elizabeth I is crowned Queen of England.	**1559** Twm is 29 years old when he obtains a pardon from Elizabeth I. He resumes his own name of Thomas Jones and becomes a country squire and a distinguished heraldic bard.	**1566** James I born to Mary Queen of Scots and Darnley.
1559 Elizabeth grants amnesty.		**1587** Mary Queen of Scots executed.
		1603 Elizabeth I died childless.
	1609 (79 years old) Thomas Jones dies.	**1603** James I crowned King of England.

Verses of the Mari Lwyd

O dyma ni'n dwad
gyfeillion diniwad
i ofyn's cawn gennad
i ganu

Oh here we come
harmless friends
to ask if we may have
permission to sing

Os na fydd 'na gennad
rhowch glywad ar ganiad
pa fodd mae'r madawiad
nos heno

If we don't have permission
let us know in song
which way to leave
tonight

Mae'r Feri Lwyd yma
('n)llawn sêrs a rhubana'
mae'n werth 'chi roi gola'
'ddi gwelad

The Mari Llwyd's here
full of stars and ribbons
it's worth putting a light on
to see her

Mae'r dîsian fras felys
llawn pob math o speisus
yn drudd ac yn gostus
'Dolig yma

The rich sweet cake
full of all types of spices
is expensive and costly
this Christmas

Mae'r dîsian fras felys
yn drudd ac yn gostus.
O rannwch hi'n garcus
i'r bechgyn

The rich sweet cake
is expensive and costly
Oh share it carefully
between the boys

Os oes yma ddynion
all naddu englynion
yn rhwydd rhowch atebion
i'r cwmni

If there are any men here
who can compose poems
easily then give your answers
to the company

(Traddodiadol)

(Traditional)

Verses and tunes may vary from area to area, the ones given here are representative of those in the parish of Llangynwyd, where an unbroken tradition exists of the Mari Lwyd. They were given by Dafydd Dafis, Maesteg, shortly before he passed away.

Heraldic Visitation of the counties of Carmarthen, Pembroke and Cardigan

SIR ABERTEIFI. PLWYF PADARN O DWYNN.[8]

PLANT y Dafydd ap Gruffydd voel val or blaen—[1]Davydd Moethe; [2]Gruffydd ap Dafydd.

Mam yrhain Katrin v̄ Syr Elidir ddu ap Elidir ap Rys.

Plant Davydd Moethe—Rys Moethe.

Ar Davydd lwn a briododd Krisli v̄ Sir Gruffydd Lloyd marchog ag afrossai o'r blaen geda Syr Gei de Breian Arglwydd Talachern.([9])

Plant Rys Moethe—Rys Moethe

Mam Rys—merch aeres Llewelyn ap Ieuan vwya ap Ieuan ap Rys ap Llowdden.

Plant Rys Moethe—Howel Moethe

Mam Howel Marged v̄ Syr Bryan de Harley, arglwydd Bromptyn Bryan ([10]) ap Syr Robart Harle.

Mam hono .... merch a koeres Howel ap David ap Owen gethin ap Owen ap Kriadog ap Gwilim Meurig.

Plant Madog ap Howel Moethe—David ap Madog, Rys ap Madog—merched Marged gwraig Ffylib Lloyd.

Mam yrhain Elen v̄ ag aeres Rys Moethe ap Ieuan Lloyd ap Ieuan ap Gruffydd hir ap Gruffydd ap David ap Gruffydd voel.

Plant David ap Madog—[1]John, [2]Rys [3]John [4]Lewys Mastr off Arts; [5]Roegiar, [6]Richiart; merched Katrin gwraig Lewys ab Ffylib.

Mam hono Elinor Herbert v̄ Syr Roegiar Herbet o Fyrton.

Plant Howel: Madog, a merched ī Marged gwraig John Kredog o Newtyn ap John Kradog: Ai vab oedd Syr Richiart Newtyn Arglwydd Chiff Justus o Loegr.([11]) Ai vab yntau Syr John Newtyn len, ai vab yntau Richiart Newtyn Ar.

Katrin yr ail a briododd Wiliam Fylib Vychan or Tylēglas ap Ffylib ap Richiart.

Y 3. Ann gwraig Syr Wiliam Klement, arglwydd Karon ([1])

4. Gwenllian gwraig Ieuan du ap Llewelyn ap Rydderch, ag wedi hyn i Gruffydd ap Llewelyn Kaplan.

Mam yrhain Sioned v̄ Wiliam ap Llewelyn ap Howel o'r Peutun.

Mam yrhain Siwann v̄ ag aeres Lewys ap Morgan ap Llewelyn ap Gruffydd vachan ap David vongam ap David ap Meurig koch.

Mam hono Angharad v̄ Gwilim ap Llewelyn vachan.

Plant John ap David Tomas [b]. ([1]) Johns o Borth y Ffynnon

Mam Tomas—Katrin [b]. v̄ Mredydd ap Ieuan ap Robert.

Arvau Tomas Johns hwnn yw pais Gwaithvoed

Dated the 30 dai off Dessember Anō R. R. Elsbeth 31 Anō Domēi 1588.

Resēved off "THOMAS JONES of Ffowntaen gat"

Vignette from the pedigree of Richard Prise of Gogerthan and Gwen Prise his wife

APPENDIX A5 (b)

Pedigree of Wm. Herbert, Earl of Pembroke

Wm Herbert Earl of Penbrook maried Ann
D. to Sir Water Devray Knt
Wm Herbert Earl of Penbrook & Huntington
maried Mary D. & coh. of Sir Richd Wodvile
Earle of Rivers
Elizabeth D. & coh. of Wm Earle of Penbrook
& Huntington maried Charles Somerset
Earle of Wosder.
Henry Somerset Earle of Wosster maried
Isabel the dau of Sir Antony Brown Knt
Visct of Mountague
Wm Somerset Earl of Worcester maried
Christian D. of Edwd Lord Northumberland
added in later ink
p. 68–78 Edwd Somerset Lord Privie Seale Earl
of Worcester & . . . . living 1612 married
. . . . . the da. of . . . . . Hastings Earl of Huntington
Henry Lord Herbert Marques of Worcester mar
rid Ann the dau. of . . . . . .

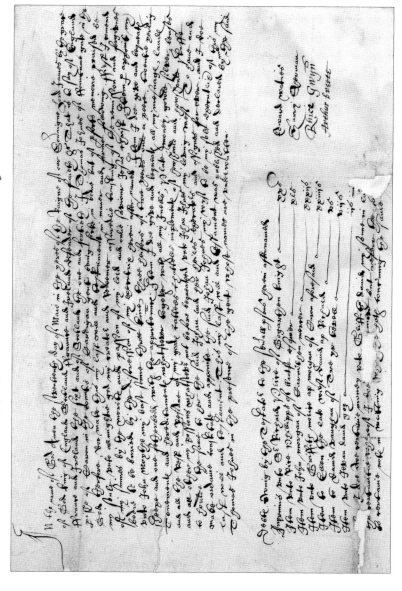

Copy of Thomas Jones's Will (2nd part)

Copy of Thomas Jones's Will (3rd part)

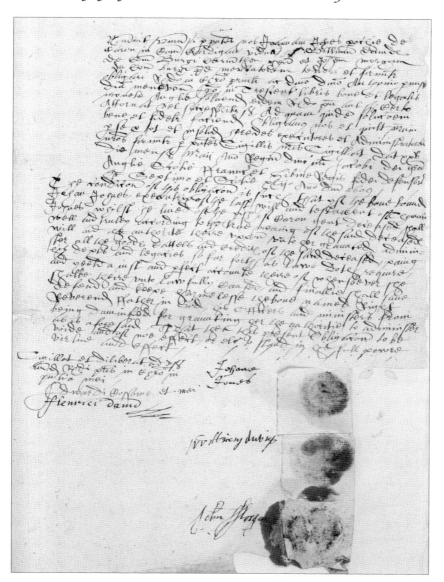

Translation of Thomas Jones's Will

Ewyllys, Thomas Johns   Will of Thomas Johns

(Twm Siôn Cati)

In the name of God Amen the seventeenth day of Maie in the yeres of the Raigne of our Sov(er)aigne Lord James by the grace of God King of England Scotland Fraunce and Ireland defender of the faieth etc That is to say of England France and Ireland the sixt and of Scotland the one and fortieth. I Thomas Johnes of Fountaine gate in the p(ar)ishe of Caron in the countie of Cardigan gent being sicke in bodie but of p(er)fecte memorie praised be God therefore, doe make this my last will and testament in maner and forme following. First I comend my soule unto allmightie god my creator and Redeemer assurredlie trusting of the remission and forgivnes of my sinners by the merites and passion of my lord and onlie saviour Jesus christ, Item I appoint my bodie to be buried by the discression of my executrix herein after named. Item I doe give and bequeth unto John Moythe my base sonne three kine, three heifers of twoe yeeres ould a peece twentie yerling sheepe and one fetherbedd with the appurtenances. Item I doe give and bequeath all my mesuages, landes tenements and hereditamentes whatsoever together with all my Juells, Plate, money, gowld, silver, leases and all the Rest and Residue of my goodes cattels chattels implements of howshould and howshould stuffe and all other my poss(ess)ions whatsoever not before bequeathed unto Johan Johnes my loving wief. To have and to houlde the same to her the said Johan and her heires executors and assignes forever. And I doe make ordaine constitute and appointe the said Johan Johnes my wyfe to be my sole executrix of this my last will and testament. This my last will and testament was published and declares by me the said Thomas Johnes in the presence of the gent whose names are underwritten.

Edward waites
Harry Sherman
Rhice Gwyn
Arthur breece

Inventory of Thomas Jones's Will

SD/1609/20
Inventory (1)

The Inventorie of all the goodes catells and chattels of Thomas Johnes of Fountaine gate in the parishe of Caron in the countie of Cardigan gent late deceassed

Inprimis of kine fiftie and one price xv s peece	xxxviii li
Item of yewes weathers and yerling sheepe	
nine score at iis vid a peece	xxii l x s
Item of lambs fourscore and three price xii d a peece	iiii li iii s
Item of oxen xviteen price xx s a peece	xvi li
Item nine beastes of three yere owld price xs a peece	iiii li xs
Item thirteen beastes of twoe yeres owld price vis viiid a peece	iiii vi s viii d
Item eighteene of beastes being twelvemonth owld	
Price iii s iiii d a peece	iii li
Item five woorking nagges price xii s iiii d a peece	iii li vi s viii d
Item one gelding price	xl s
Item three owld mares price xs a peece	xxx s
Item twoe cowltes of twoe yere owld price xs a peece	xx s
Item one fyllie of twealvemoneth owld price	v s
Item in plate	xiii li xiii s viii d
Item in pewter vessels of all sortes	iii li
Item in Brasen vessels and kitching implimentes	iii li
Item in Bedsteedes and woodden vessells	x ls
Item nineteene fetherbeddes with their app(er)tenances	xv l
Item in Naperie	xls
Sommis	139 £-5s

Pedigree of Sir Walter Rise of Newton in Dinevowr

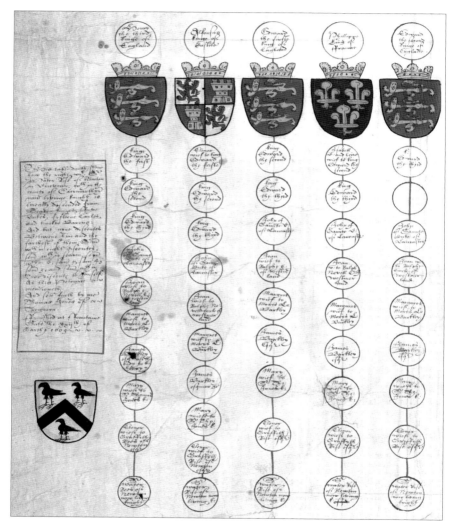

Margaret Isaac's books are inspired by the Welsh landscape and are rooted in place. Her stories are told with a passion for the culture and history of Wales. She believes this is a wonderful inheritance to be passed down to the Welsh and other Celtic peoples who now inhabit Wales and many other corners of the world.

BY THE SAME AUTHOR

Tales of Gold
1999. ISBN 0 9537267 0 3
Five short stories of Caves, Gold and Magic.

Sir Gawain and the Green Knight
2000. ISBN 0 9537267 4 6
It is Christmas time in King Arthur's court. Gawain, Arthur's nephew, accepts a mortal challenge from an enchanted giant.

Nia and the Magic of the Lake
2000. ISBN 0 9537267 3 8
The story of a growing friendship between a boy and a girl set against the backdrop of the legend of Llyn y Fan Fach.

Rhiannon's Way
2002. ISBN 0 9537267 8 9
Caradog, a Celtic chieftain, has been captured by the Romans. His daughter Rhiannon sets out to rescue him with the help of her friend Brychan and a little help from a magic pony and a magic mirror.

The Tale of Twm Siôn Cati
2005. ISBN 0 9548940 1 4
Stories based on traditional tales of the famous Welsh folk hero.

Lake Stories of Wales, *Shadows in the Waters*
2008. ISBN 978 0 9548940 6 1
Five short stories based on lakes in South Wales.

Storïau Llynnoedd Cymru, *Cysgodion yn y Dyfroedd*
2008. ISBN 978 0 9548940 7 8

*Designed and published by Apecs Press
on the four hundredth anniversary of the death of
Thomas Jones of Tregaron alias Twm Siôn Cati.*

Printed by Gwasg Dinefwr.

The edition is limited to four hundred copies.

Copy number

162